Scriptural Re
for Primary Schools

How to Share and Explore Sacred Texts and their Stories

Anne Margaret Moseley

Research Tutor at Oxford Centre for Mission Studies

Educational Consultant at Rose Castle Foundation

GROVE BOOKS LIMITED

RIDLEY HALL RD CAMBRIDGE CB3 9HU

Contents

AADE
Anglican Association of Directors of Education

First Impression July 2022
ISSN 2041-0964
ISBN 978 1 78827 249 0

Introduction to Scriptural Reasoning

1

I wonder if you have ever been to an event that opened your eyes to something that you had never seen before? One that set you off on a new journey of discovery, or turned your world upside down and challenged previously-held attitudes and beliefs? This is what happened to me at a Religious Education (RE) conference organized in 2008 by the Christian Muslim Forum.[1] For the first time I, as a Christian educator, found myself in a context where I felt able to talk openly about my faith in the company of fellow educators who happened to be Muslims. We shared insights about the impact faith had on our professional lives and explored stories of our experiences in schools. This common ground enabled us to feel confident talking together as people of faith in a secular working environment. The conference had created a space that felt safe for us to reflect on our experiences and ask questions in a way that was honest, respectful and engaging. It was at this conference that I first experienced scriptural reasoning, and I was hooked.

What is Scriptural Reasoning?

Scriptural reasoning is an approach to learning that brings sacred texts from different religious traditions alongside each other.[2] Its focus is on developing an understanding of religion, as experienced by participants, through an open and honest discussion, where the sacred texts are at the heart of the dialogue. It originated in an academic context in the 1990s and can trace its roots back to the work of Peter Ochs, a Jewish scholar, and David Ford, a Christian theologian, but is now widely used in the public space.

Scriptural Reasoning first originated within the Abrahamic traditions, where there are many natural connections between the texts and the process of reading them. In the Jewish tradition, there is a practice known as *chavruta,* which invites a shared reading of a text in order to call out meaning together through study, analysis and discussion. This style of learning is experienced by Christians when churches run *Bible* study groups to help believers apply biblical principles to Christian living. However, it was when scriptural reasoning began to include the study of Islamic texts, and a third voice was brought into the conversation, that it really developed its distinctive momentum. Koshul and Kepnes note the significance of the term *aql* (thinking or reasoning), which is used over thirty-six times in the *Qur'an,* implying that within the Islamic narrative there is also the possibility of constructive dialogue and reasoning with others.[3] This opened the possibility of a three-part dialogue, or trialogue, that welcomed diverse styles of reading and discussion, thus opening a more nuanced conversation that honoured difference.

At the heart of scriptural reasoning there are three core principles or learning outcomes:

- *Learning and understanding*—as participants learn about other religious traditions and worldviews, they are better able to understand their own.
- *Exploring differences*—as participants apply the principles of mutual critical engagement, they become better able to disagree well.
- *Building friendships*—as participants meet together and draw on shared wisdom, new relationships are built and prejudices challenged.

Whilst there are many different expressions of scriptural reasoning, a typical encounter would bring together members from different faith communities to form a collaborative community of inquiry. It is usual to share three sacred texts alongside each other, as this provides different perspectives around a single theme. Each text would be read out in turn by a community member, who then goes on to explain what it means and why it is significant to them. They speak from their own experiences, not necessarily as expert theologians but rather as members of a particular faith tradition. There follows a time for questions, answers and small group discussions to help participants develop a fuller understanding of the lived experiences of people taking part.

Scriptural reasoning has now grown into a global network of practitioners who have applied the principles in both academic and non-academic contexts. It has developed to incorporate other religions, worldviews and philosophical positions, even those without sacred texts of their own. The important aspect of the texts used in scriptural reasoning is that they should be significant *carriers of meaning* for the participants.

As a primary RE specialist, I could see the potential for using this approach in the classroom. Although scriptural reasoning had begun within faith communities, I became aware that it had been adapted for use in prison communities and the NHS using an approach that applied story and drama. I began to see how this might translate into the primary classroom, given that story is such a significant part of the primary curriculum.

I could see this working particularly well in a topic I regularly covered, on 'How the world began.' The content of these sessions involved comparing stories from different religious and cultural backgrounds and exploring a variety of perspectives on the origins of the universe. I was struck by the depth of insight and the quality of dialogue that came out of these sessions. However, my limited knowledge of other traditions and worldviews made it difficult for me to clarify the appropriateness of some of the pupils' observations. It appeared to me that this encounter was similar to that experienced through scriptural reasoning, the difference being that in the classroom there were no faith representatives or faith guides to engage with, and contribute to, the pupils' ideas.

Why is Scriptural Reasoning an Appropriate Model?

At about the same time as the Christian Muslim conference was taking place, I had been working in my school to develop a global citizenship curriculum. I wanted to take seriously government guidance on the duty to promote community cohesion.[4] Schools were being encouraged to think about how children could learn to live well with difference and contribute to their local community as UK citizens and also members of a wider global community.

In my own school context, many of the pupils had an awareness of global issues, yet I noticed they had very little knowledge of the diverse expressions of what being British looked like beyond our small, leafy English town. After attending training with what was then the Bradford School Linking Network, our school set up a partnership with an inner-city school just a few miles away and began a one-year project, following the model set up by the Linking Network.[5] I wanted to use this opportunity to focus specifically on developing intercultural competencies with the pupils.

The pupils accepted differences as a creative part of the learning process

During the school linking project, the pupils enjoyed learning from each other, accepting differences as a creative part of the learning process.[6] They particularly enjoyed visiting each other's schools, where they encountered a warm reception and began to recognize that all schools were not the same. There was a certain amount of nervousness at first but, as the year progressed, I observed that pupils had become more comfortable working in an unfamiliar environment and also more reflective in the way they processed these encounters.

It was clear to me that the school linking project resonated with the underlying principles of scriptural reasoning. However, this approach, which was rooted in the desire to develop intercultural competencies, did not recognize the potential for inter-religious competencies or a worldviews perspective. I began to wonder if an approach that applied stories as carriers of meaning to the practice of scriptural reasoning might help pupils to develop a greater awareness not only of cultural identity but also religious identity. This is where the seed for my research began to take root.[7]

I was already aware of a significant body of knowledge that highlighted the potential for using RE to develop intercultural competencies. Robert Jackson, through his work with the Council of Europe, produced advice and a range of reports that identified how these two areas could be linked.[8] I have since built on this work to explore an approach, based on scriptural reasoning principles, which considers not only intercultural competencies but also the possibility of inter-religious and worldview competencies. This book seeks to share some of the findings and insights that came out of the research, in the hope that it will inspire others to explore how scriptural reasoning encounters might benefit the pupils in their own school contexts.

Questions for Reflection

- In what way does your curriculum give pupils an understanding of their place within the UK and global community?
- Are there any examples of intercultural learning that already take place in your school?

Learning Through the Lens of Story

2

At this point in history, fake news and misinformation are eroding confidence in what is true and what can be believed. With so many contested narratives in the public space, we find it difficult to know where to turn. I would like to suggest that our sacred stories can provide an environment where the search for meaning is more significant than the search for absolute truth.

Wired for Story

There is something about the human condition that is wired for story. From an early age children practise telling stories about themselves in order to make sense of their environment. It is wonderful to listen to playground games, as children navigate imaginary worlds and build narratives together which not only develop language but also a sense of their identity and where they fit into the world.

This was highlighted for me many years ago when my son convinced his nursery teachers that he had visited Africa. We had not; however, he had watched *The Jungle Book* and had also fallen in love with elephants through the books he had encountered. In his mind he was drawing together information from the outside world and creating a story where he was the hero and the adventurer. So convincing was his account that his teachers assumed he must have truly been there. In acting out and telling his story, he was processing the information available as well as experimenting with who he was and how he connected with his environment. This was not something he had been taught; it was an innate instinct to try to make sense of his world through his imagination.

Understanding Our Place in the World Through Story

It is from this early age that we begin to develop a self-narrative about who we are and how we fit within the social contexts in which we find ourselves. We develop an internal account that puts the self centre-stage. It tries to interpret the actions of those around us in the light of lived experiences already encountered. We take in information through our senses, interpreting it to reconstruct in our own minds a constantly changing world. Ricoeur, a well-regarded twentieth-century philosopher in the hermeneutic tradition, describes this process of interpretation as being like landing in the middle of a play and trying to make sense of what is going on:

> To interpret meaning is, for Ricoeur, to arrive in the middle of an exchange which has already begun and in which we seek to orientate ourselves in order to make some new sense of it.[9]

This notion is helpful in that it enables us to explore meaning, whilst recognizing we can only see partially. We look for evidence to confirm our understanding as we encounter something new or different.

I would argue that it is at these points of unfamiliarity and ambiguity that it is possible for new learning and creative thinking to be birthed. Furthermore, story is a particularly helpful vehicle for this type of learning. It is in the process of reviewing and refining insights that we begin to open and explore new meaning. Done in isolation, this can leave us vulnerable to our own prejudices and bias. It is when we allow others to interact with and challenge our narratives that we build a fuller understanding of the world in which we live.

Stories provide a space in which we can explore our prejudices and biases within an environment which does not threaten our identities. As we are invited into the story, we find ourselves exploring what is happening through the eyes of the characters. The very fact that most story arcs include a problem to be solved and a new meaning to be found enables the reader to expect a change in their own understanding as part of the process of the encounter. In scriptural reasoning, we are looking to facilitate this type of learning. Through an encounter with a story, pupils are invited into a place that will challenge preconceptions, yet in a way that feels safe and does not threaten their identities. At the same time, these encounters, when experienced in community, can allow internal narratives to be challenged as new information is incorporated through the perspectives of others. Voices come from within the stories but also from those new insights expressed by fellow participants who are on a journey of discovery together.

Holding Meaning Within a Story

The way our brains process language is a fascinating and much-researched topic. We are creatures that enjoy the search for meaning. We like to look for cause and effect, to create models of the world that order the confusion. We like to ask questions to clarify what we think and believe to be true; we also seek to fill in the gaps so as to form an impression and run a narrative along the lines of our past experiences.

For example, if I were to ask you to tell a story in its very simplest form from just three words, I wonder what story you would create? The story is: tiger—man—tiger. I wonder what images came into your mind:

- What did your tiger look like?
- Where was the tiger?
- What was the nature of its encounter with the man?
- Did the man disappear or are there now two tigers?

The pupils who took part in this activity were often surprised to hear many different versions of the story as they shared from their own imaginations. This approach creates an atmosphere where hidden meaning is expected, even desired, and makes stories a very helpful place for pupils to explore different interpretations.

Stories are also helpful in that they are easy to remember and can be retold with accuracy. The psychologist Frederick Bartlett, in his classic 1932 experiment, found that brains did something rather interesting.[10] As stories were retold over time, the core elements remained the same but the peripheral details changed. The core meaning was being remembered and could be recalled with significant accuracy, whilst the missing information could be refined and retold to adapt to different audiences. This suggests that story is a reliable way to communicate narratives over time and across cultures, and is therefore an effective method of shaping and passing on group identity and values. This clearly has implications for the transmission of religious traditions and worldviews. Through story, it is possible to bring together historical tradition, critical reason and shared personal experiences, in a way that builds community and shared identity.

Sacred texts are a powerful example of group stories because they bring together historical memories that have been used to pass on meaning and are thus laden with significance. Such texts come with authority because they are considered to contain wisdom from God, which can be relevant across time and cultures. Faith communities can approach them with confidence, as a way of finding meaning and significance within their own faith groups. However, these texts can also be helpful for those of no faith, who are looking to learn from the history of wisdom literature.

The Search for Meaning

Many religious traditions have easily identifiable sacred texts that carry significant meaning for them such as the *Bible*, the *Qur'an*, the *Torah*, the *Guru Granth Sahib* and the *Vedas*. These sacred texts are regularly used within the RE curriculum, but there are other sources which are less widely recognized and hold the potential for exploring worldviews through the vehicle of story. Wisdom is shared in Chinese culture through traditional folk tales; *Aesop's Fables*, which were first told in ancient Greece, still carry meaning today; whilst the Buddhist tradition draws wisdom from the *Jataka* tales. All these texts can be significant carriers of meaning. They are narratives that shape the values and beliefs of individuals, as well as texts which are used to pass on wisdom.

Whilst these stories are useful in exploring meaning, they are also living texts and actively used by individuals for building up personal knowledge. It is this aspect of the lived experience of faith that is important in the process of scriptural reasoning. When we come together to share these narratives or carriers of meaning, we are looking to understand how wisdom is applied and how meaning can be interpreted through the lived experiences of others.

The scriptural reasoning approach can be relevant whether children are religious or non-religious. When we put these stories alongside each other, the aim is to share insights and understanding from a personal perspective. As we encounter the texts together through dialogue, it is possible to gain wisdom about our own understanding of the world through these encounters, whilst the texts can also become carriers of meaning for all those taking part. They become woven into our shared experiences of life, part of a new story we are telling together about our lived experiences.

Weaving Meaning in the Company of Others

Traditional interpretations of sacred texts are often explored within faith communities, under the guidance of trained religious leaders or theologians. Scriptural reasoning, however, offers the opportunity for meaning to be explored through the eyes of those outside our faith community. When we choose to share our stories in the company of others, we see different perspectives and new insights can emerge that might not have been seen within our own faith communities. Working alongside others, we not only develop an understanding of their perspectives, but we are also more able fully to understand our own.

Working alongside others' perspectives, we are more able fully to understand our own perspective

This concept of developing a shared understanding of the world has been identified by Hans-Georg Gadamer, another twentieth-century philosopher.[11] He suggests that a 'fusion of horizons' becomes possible, as people come together to share from their experiences and explain the encounter. Whilst we may each have a deep knowledge of the world, what we have experienced is only a partial view. If we want to gain a more detailed understanding, we will need to enlist the help of others who see the world from different perspectives. Through collaborative dialogue, it is possible to develop a shared understanding of the world as it is seen from different angles.

You may be familiar with the parable of the blind men and the elephant that originated in India. It describes how a group of blind men first encountered an elephant. One of them felt the ear and explained an elephant was fanlike, another felt the leg and believed the elephant was like a tree trunk, whilst the third felt the trunk and described the elephant as snakelike. Each one only saw part of the picture. But as the three of them began to talk together they developed a much fuller understanding of what the elephant looked like. Each one thought that their own interpretation was complete. It was only when the three perspectives were put alongside each other that they could see more fully what the whole elephant looked like.

Whilst scriptural reasoning originated in an academic context, I believe that it can be effectively adapted for the primary classroom with an emphasis on stories as carriers of meaning—a very natural place for pupils to search for meaning and explore their place within the world.

Scriptural reasoning involves story *sharing* rather than simply storytelling. As we bring our sacred stories alongside each other and embark on such story sharing, we build a fuller picture of the world, as seen through the eyes of others, gaining alternative perspectives to our familiar narratives.

Stories provide a particularly effective vehicle for doing this as they articulate deep-rooted values and beliefs, which carry meaning not only for individuals but also for faith communities and wider global traditions.

Questions for Reflection

- Can you tell the tiger-man-tiger story to someone else and then ask them to tell their story? How is it different?
- Can you find some time to observe children playing in the playground or at home with colleagues, family members or acquaintances? What do you notice about collaborative meaning-making through imaginary play?
- If you have any friends from different religious traditions and worldviews, can you ask them what their favourite story is and why it is special to them?

3 Exploring Difference Through Dialogue

There are many ways for us to talk together: times when we communicate information simply as facts to be shared; times when we debate and argue to discern the rights and wrongs in a situation. There are other times when we have open conversations where collaborative joint decision-making is the aim. However, there is another way of talking that helps us to learn and understand from each other through an inquiry-based dialogue.

The example that comes to my mind as I consider this type of communication is the story of the disciples on the road to Emmaus. In Luke 24 we read about how two disciples on their journey to Emmaus were walking and talking with each other, discussing everything that had happened in Jerusalem. As they were talking, a third voice was introduced into the conversation—that of Jesus, as he came alongside them and started asking them questions. They recounted what had happened, reflecting on what they had experienced and been taught in the past. As they were walking and talking together, they were able to process what they had witnessed and approach things through fresh eyes. In fact, the Bible tells us they had a profound moment of recognition of Jesus himself.

It is this style of communication that develops learning and understanding in a way that fits well with a scriptural reasoning approach. It allows lived experiences, in all their richness, to be part of the dialogue, building connection through a shared experience in which meaning is explored together. As schools begin to develop a worldview approach to RE, in the light of the Commission on Religious Education (CoRE) report, this style of dialogue, as exemplified in the scriptural reasoning approach, is particularly relevant for our pupils.[12]

Developing Mutual Critical Engagement Through Dialogue

As outlined above, this style of dialogue is different from much of the talk which takes place in the classroom. David Ford, one of the originators of scriptural reasoning, suggests that this type of interaction could be described as 'mutual critical engagement':

> Secular societies have generally failed to mobilize religious resources for public wisdom and peace. Religions have often reacted against them,

> faced with a choice between assimilation or confrontation. But there is another possibility: mutually critical engagement among all participants aimed at transforming the public space for the better.[13]

Following my experience of working on the school linking project, I believed the type of dialogue outlined by David Ford could be applied in a way that built on primary pupils' ability to engage with difference. This mode of understanding does not look for consensus, or spark conflict, but allows respectful honest engagement, where difference can be seen as an integral part of the encounter.

In order to provide an environment for pupils to develop this critical engagement, I developed a framework which consisted of three key attitudes. I wanted to create a place where pupils could demonstrate Respect towards each other, be Open to new ideas whilst confident in their own position and be Curious. To highlight these desired attitudes, I developed an acronym and taught the pupils the importance of 'attitudes that ROC': that is, attitudes that demonstrated Respect, Openness and Curiosity.

Respect—Look Again

The first attitude we talked about was that of respect. The etymological root of 'respect' can be found in the Latin *spectre*, which means 'to look at,' and *re*, which means 'back' or 'again.' I found that the pupils I worked with in schools demonstrated respect for both the visiting storytellers and the sacred texts they were reading from. Pupils frequently commented on the importance of respect:

> I knew it was from a different book, so I had to respect their religion. (George)

Openness—Listen Carefully

The second attitude we talked about was that of being open and willing to learn something new, something that had not previously been apparent. Most of us, most of the time, only see part of a bigger picture. Allowing an openness with others, especially those from different faith perspectives, can be an enriching experience which enables our understanding to grow. Being willing to listen and see things from a different perspective helps us to develop a critical perspective that can not only challenge what others are saying, but also our own perceptions and biases. This attitude was observed during our work in schools:

I have heard another story before and that is different and so I have to try and move that out of the way so that I can listen and compare them to each other. (Mark)

Curiosity—Ask Questions

The third attitude we talked about was that of curiosity. We found that those pupils who demonstrated curiosity were the ones who discovered most. This is not really surprising, but it is important to note:

- So, I didn't know what was happening, so I was a bit curious like you said yesterday. (Paul)
- I thought it was very powerful and it made me feel very interested. (Mark)
- I really wanted to know what happened at the end. (Sumera)

We found that most pupils were full of questions, not only about the stories but also about the lived experiences of the participants. However, for some of the pupils these encounters were not easy, their comments suggesting a reluctance to explore the ideas of others. Being aware of this was important for facilitators as we tried to find ways to support those pupils, enabling them to feel confident to talk honestly in unfamiliar encounters.

Developing Honest Talk

Alongside these 'attitudes that ROC,' we raised the importance of speaking clearly about personal values and beliefs. From my research, I found that the children who were able to state their ideas clearly and honestly benefited most from these learning encounters:

So, I was thinking about what they're thinking and how strong it is to them; and it helps me to understand how strong I can be of my faith. (Lucy)

In the classroom, pupils often feel the need to provide the answers they believe their teachers are expecting. In these scriptural reasoning encounters, it was important for pupils to explore their own insights, without fear of judgement. Establishing a 'safe space' facilitated their ability to bear witness to their own experiences and develop ownership of their values and beliefs. To enable this personal witness and ownership, it was important to set up a safe space.

Whilst this style of dialogue could be appropriate across many areas of school life, I believe that it fits particularly well within the RE curriculum, effectively promoting the development of mutual critical engagement. Robert Jackson (who is widely recognized for his work in developing an interpretive approach to RE) also recognizes the importance of RE in the public space, and has highlighted the possibility of schools being a safe place for developing dialogue that respects difference. In his book, *Signposts,* which makes a number of recommendations for the RE community, he identifies the significant part religious communities can play in developing understanding of difference:

> The recommendations encourage links between schools and their wider community, including religious communities and non-religious organizations, as a means to learning, to help develop a culture of living together despite differences and to link local issues with global ones.[14]

Jackson identifies a way in which the RE curriculum can offer a space for religious and non-religious communities to be invited into the school environment, which can enrich not only the pupils' learning but also model, for those outside the school, what learning to live well with difference looks like.

Questions for Reflection

- Can you think of a time when your perceptions were changed through conversations with someone from a different worldview?
- If you think the 'attitudes that ROC' approaches would be useful in your context, how would you apply them?
- How could you begin to reach out to members of faith communities represented in your area?

4 A Place to Build Friendships

I wonder what images come to mind as you reflect on your own experiences of listening to stories? Perhaps images of a fireside or bedtime, images of people gathered in a warm, welcoming place, friends and family drawing close together to learn and reflect on the messages together. Whatever you imagine, it is likely that you associate it with a feeling of safety or security. The concept of a safe space was something I was keen to investigate further as part of my research on the impact of scriptural reasoning in the classroom. I quickly realized that creating a space of safety involved creating a place of hospitality. I wanted to find a way to recreate this place of hospitality in a school setting—somewhere that would facilitate learning and understanding and could build friendships, whilst allowing for different interpretations to be respected and different worldviews to be critically explored. I began to see how establishing a temporary space in the classroom could set a tone that would allow the rules of engagement to be different from those normally experienced in the classroom. This was where the concept of a story tent began to emerge.

Being in a Tent

David Ford applies the imagery of dwelling spaces to differentiate between different types of religious encounters. The first, *the house,* he suggests, is where faith is worked out alongside fellow believers. Places such as churches, synagogues and mosques are the homes in which faith is worked out with like-minded believers. The second, *the campus,* he describes as shared ground where people of many faiths and none learn together. This could be an academic or public space where beliefs can be contested. The third, *the tent,* suggests a temporary space. It is not a permanent home or an academic institution but rather a place where expectations are different:

> It is of a different order to a house or campus, suggesting (at least in our culture), a place that is not one's permanent home, and not in competition with the others as religious or academic institutions.[15]

It is in such a tent space that the emphasis is on building friendship, through an atmosphere of hospitality and trust. It ties in with ancient traditions of welcoming the stranger and seeking to serve them first. Putting the stranger, wherever they came from, at the centre and providing for their needs, was offered as a mark of respect and shared humanity. At times, these could prove to be risky encounters, yet there was a cultural understanding that respect should be offered and hospitality honoured. It is this kind of environment that we tried to create in schools, a unique place that required an intensified respectful attitude.

Scriptural reasoning sits best within this tent space, and is the model that was key to the development of our schools' work. We sought to create a hospitable space, where friendships could be made through relaxed encounters, as well as a liminal space, where something of the sacred could be experienced. This in-between place became an interpretative space, where all were welcome and all voices could be heard.

As we explored how to present this in schools, we wanted to turn the metaphor of the tent into an embodied representation of a space that was distinct from the classroom. Therefore, as part of the scriptural reasoning encounter, we physically put up a gazebo in the classroom. This enabled us to create a space where pupils could become both guests of the storytellers, who would share from their traditions, yet also hosts, with their own stories to share. The tent became a temporary place where hospitality was offered and something of the human condition experienced.

Being Hospitable

This concept of a tent of hospitality can be found in the biblical narrative. In Genesis 18, we see how Abraham entertains three strangers in a tent, strangers (who are angels) bringing good news that he and his wife will give birth to a son. In Exodus 40, we see how God instructs Moses to set up the tent of meeting: a holy place where God himself dwells with his people. These accounts are relevant across the Abrahamic traditions and demonstrate that the tent can be understood as a space that can be both sacred and hospitable. The tent is a place of nourishment for the common good, a liminal place where all can experience something spiritual, whether or not they fully appreciate the significance.

The tent can be understood as a space that can be both sacred and hospitable

Having provided the tent space, we also wanted to signal that this physical space was different from the normal classroom environment. This space required a heightened level of respect and openness to the ideas of others we might not agree with. To make this place feel safe, we developed some guidelines for dialogue. At the start of any new encounter, we would go through these guidelines so that pupils had a clear set of shared behavioural expectations. We wanted to create a framework that was age appropriate and would help primary pupils to talk honestly about their lived experiences, values and worldviews, within a context that placed difference at the heart of the conversation.

Guidelines for Dialogue

- *Respect other viewpoints, even if you disagree.*
- *Be honest about what you say and explain why.*
- *Speak positively about what you think and not negatively about what someone else thinks.*
- *Look out for similarities and differences.*
- *Make every effort to get along with everyone.*
- *If you feel uncomfortable you can say STOP, and we will stop.*

Setting these expectations at the start of the scriptural reasoning encounter enabled pupils to acknowledge and understand the boundaries. Comments from Jamila are indicative of the level of comfort pupils felt as they engaged with other religions:

> I think it is really important to never force people to do that religion, I think you should let them decide but I think you should still tell them about it and let them decide in the end. (Jamila)

Jamila was from a religiously conservative Muslim family and yet she felt comfortable and confident to talk openly about her beliefs, and was willing to listen to other perspectives without her identity being threatened.

Being Together

Scriptural reasoning allows participants to journey alongside each other in a way that holds conversation as the focus, rather than any change in beliefs. The power of contact to build bridges and overcome misunderstandings has been widely researched. This aspect of bridge-building was central to the principles I wanted to create in the classroom and so I turned to the work of Gordon Allport and his contact theory (1954).[16]

Contact theory recognizes the value of diversity and of developing meaningful encounters in safe spaces, where religious and cultural differences can be explored. In his intergroup contact hypothesis, Allport identifies four key conditions required for successful encounters:

- Equal status.
- Intergroup cooperation.
- Common goals.
- Support by social and institutional authorities.

There has been a growing awareness of the significance of contact theory in the RE curriculum, and it has been of particular interest to the *Shared Space* research project developed through the National Association of Teachers of Religious Education (based at Bristol University).[17]

I considered it important to embed these principles into the activities that we undertook and emphasized that all voices should be respected if not agreed with. The planned activities highlighted working in groups collaboratively, and there was always an adult present to facilitate each activity. In being aware of these principles, we tried to ensure that pupils felt that they could be honest about their experiences whilst remaining a valued part of the group, so that they could not only find out more about other beliefs and values, but also have space to reflect on their own identity and worldview.

The tent space that I have described in this chapter has become significant in the work that I have subsequently developed, particularly the concept of creating a pop-up space for encounters where difference and diversity can be celebrated. The tent space becomes a place of hospitality where people feel comfortable in the company of others, as well as facilitating the third learning outcome of scriptural reasoning—that of building friendships.

This moveable space has the potential to offer a context in which people who hold different values and beliefs can meet together, share stories, explore differences and realize that their shared humanity and genuine differences can be held together at the same time. When this space is set up well, with accepted rules for dialogue and Allport's conditions for contact, I believe it enables the possibility of building bridges and developing significant friendships that might not have been possible before.

Questions for Reflection

- Do you feel that the descriptions of the three different meeting places are helpful—the house, the campus and the tent?
- How could you create a safe space in your school, where these types of encounters could take place?

5 The Importance of Identity

We live in a world that is becoming increasingly polarized, where fear of others is driving communities apart, with like-minded people drawing together around cultural, religious and political identities. Now is the time for us to be developing encounters that build trust, through open dialogue about things that matter, where religion is explicitly part of the conversation. Identity, otherness and community are all three important elements of scriptural reasoning encounters and will be considered in turn, whilst recognizing that they are all interlinked.

Who Am I?—A Sense of Identity

I have become increasingly aware, as I allow myself to become immersed in the scriptural reasoning approach, that I am constantly narrating a story in my own head; a story that is interpreting and assimilating my experiences in the light of what I have known from the past. I am telling a story where I am the central participant and others are invited in, informing me of what the world is like. When I encounter people like me, I will assume that all the world is like me. When I encounter those who hold different perspectives, I begin to think more carefully about my fundamental core beliefs and values. My story is shaped by my own beliefs and values, whilst others are invited in to share what the world is like to them. These new insights can then be woven into my own story and become part of who I am, even though I might not agree with everything that I hear. This helps to shape my very personal narrative of the world and everything in it.

Recent work carried out by the Theos think tank has highlighted that we need to be aware that we all hold within us viewpoints that are not neutral, but are rather shaped by a number of influences. Their recent animation, *Nobody Stands Nowhere,* suggests that we all hold worldviews that are influenced by our upbringing, environments and beliefs, whether they are religious or not.[18] Being aware of our own position can be incredibly helpful, helping us to talk openly as we encounter other people and begin to shape our personal narratives.

My experience of developing scriptural reasoning encounters in primary schools suggests that pupils have some awareness of their own position. Whilst I did not explicitly invite pupils to talk about their identity, it was clear from their interviews that pupils were able to draw from their own personal narrative as a very natural part of the conversations. It was interesting to observe a range of identity markers that pupils used. Some pupils did identify with positions of belief such as: 'I'm a Christian,' 'I'm a Muslim,' 'I believe in science'; some referred to aspects of personality such as: 'I'm shy'; while others referred to geographical identity markers such as: 'He was from Africa.'

I observed that pupils who had an awareness of their own beliefs and values, and were better able to tolerate ambiguity, were more able to hear the voices of others who held a different worldview. They had the language and vocabulary to talk about, and engage in, the conversation because of their own sense of personhood. They knew what it was like to believe in something, so they were able to talk more widely about what others believed. They knew what it was like to be culturally aware, so they could talk about culture in a broader sense. I was surprised to observe that some of the less academically able pupils performed really well in these encounters, whilst some of those who may have had better literacy and oracy skills found it harder to embrace what others believed, simply because they did not have an awareness of the concepts, or the language, to describe what they were experiencing.

Who Are You?—A Sense of Empathy

For pupils to thrive in these scriptural reasoning encounters, we found that it was important that they were not only confident of their own position and willing to talk openly about their beliefs, but also able to demonstrate empathetic responses. In their Autobiography of Intercultural Encounters (AIE) guidelines, the Council of Europe describes empathy as 'the ability to project oneself into another person's perspective and to be considerate towards their motives, opinions, ways of thinking and their feelings.'[19] There was evidence that this was happening with almost all the pupils taking part in these encounters.

These empathetic responses were particularly noticeable in the interview responses. Many of the pupils recognized that it took courage for the faith guide to go into an unfamiliar school setting, and yet it was this modelled courage that set a tone for the pupils to be honest. For example, Susan could imagine the pride that the faith guide would feel taking part in the day, but she also applied it back to an experience she remembered when starting school herself:

> I think she would be proud of herself, because she is talking about her religion to other people and there are not many people who are Jews in this school. So it's a really big thing for her because she is trying, like when we started school, we are trying to fit in so she is trying to fit in with other people as well. (Susan)

It was also interesting to see that for some children there was an empathetic response to the characters in the story. As we have discussed in chapter two, stories provide a unique invitation to enter into an imagined space. These spaces allow not only real people to be encountered but also those embedded in the stories themselves. Sumera was very concerned about the rejection that Noah was experiencing. She not only could imagine what it would have been like for him, but was also able to name the emotions:

> I felt really sad because no one was listening to Noah, but Noah was listening to God, so I felt happy about that. (Sumera)

These empathetic responses enabled the pupils to project themselves into the experiences of another—real or imagined—and connect it to their lived experiences. It became an experience of the human condition, which recognized difference but placed it in the context of a shared humanity.

Who Are We?—Building a Community Together

As a result of this coming together, we found that there was something intrinsically enjoyable about sharing time together. We found that talking openly from our lived experiences with an empathetic and open attitude began to build a sense of connection and community, for both adults and pupils alike. We found that many of the pupils who took part felt a great sense of enjoyment and positivity about learning from others and did not find it difficult to hold in tension the fact that their opinions were different. For example:

> I think it's a bit different to what I would expect it to be. I'm not like a Christian or something, I didn't really believe in it but I thought this is important to hear so I should just listen and be careful what I say. (Joy)

This was exactly the type of attitude we were hoping to develop: one where pupils could be aware of their own position and accept that others might hold different viewpoints. We were talking about stories that enabled participants to enter into a shared space that did not seek to ascertain the truth (or otherwise) of certain viewpoints, but hospitably offered different ways of understanding the world. This suggested that the scriptural reasoning approach that we were using was having a positive effect in the classroom settings.

As we built on the principles outlined in scriptural reasoning, we noticed an evolving interpretive community, one that has been highlighted by Julia Ipgrave:

> It could be said that the text gathered an interpretive community around it as the children asked and answered questions about its content and meaning.[20]

Working together, particularly in groups of threes, we found that new insights were being formed and woven into our personal narratives. Although the stories shared may not necessarily have been significant carriers of meaning for the pupils at the beginning, by the end of an encounter these stories had been woven into the pupils' personal narrative. The very fact that we had experienced sharing stories together had changed us. This change was not only experienced at a personal level; there was also something about forming an interpretive community that brought us closer together, which created a sense of *shalom* and well-being.

Questions for Reflection

- Who am I? I wonder how you would choose to describe yourself?
- Who are you? Can you think of any risky encounters (see chapter four) that have enriched your life?
- Who are we? Think of a community of which you are a part. How much do the values and beliefs within the group coincide, or diverge?

6 Conclusion

Key Principles

In the light of all that has been discussed, I want to draw out some of the key themes that have emerged from my experiences of applying scriptural reasoning principles to the primary classroom.

I have suggested that stories from sacred texts, or stories as carriers of meaning, can be a helpful vehicle for learning and understanding other perspectives with primary-aged pupils. They provide a context, which is familiar for pupils, to explore and adapt their viewpoints in a way that does not compromise their identity and, in fact, helps them to come to a fuller understanding of their own beliefs and values.

I have identified the potential for dialogue, or trialogue, that brings together three voices. This three-part encounter creates a more stable environment, with three points of reference to draw on in the process of interpreting the stories. I have noted that, when three different perspectives are brought together, it is possible for differences to be explored in a way that moves beyond binary positions and allows for a more nuanced response.

I have also explored the significance of creating the space in which scriptural reasoning encounters occur, and suggested that the concept of the tent, as outlined by David Ford, could offer a useful image of a temporary space within the school environment. This space is slightly different from that normally experienced in the classroom and offers a context in which pupils can engage respectfully in dialogue where difference is central to the encounter. It is a space for collaborative inquiry, which allows for respectful questions to be asked and mutual critical engagement to take place.

Finally, I propose an approach that encourages pupils to bring the whole of their identity into these conversations. We each have a unique set of experiences and perspectives that can, when handled sensitively, enrich learning. If we can encourage our pupils to develop the skills of respectful, open listening and the ability to share out of their own lived experiences, we can hope to build healthy communities of learning that are enabled to live well with difference.

The model below demonstrates how these principles can be put together as a framework for building scriptural reasoning encounters in primary schools:

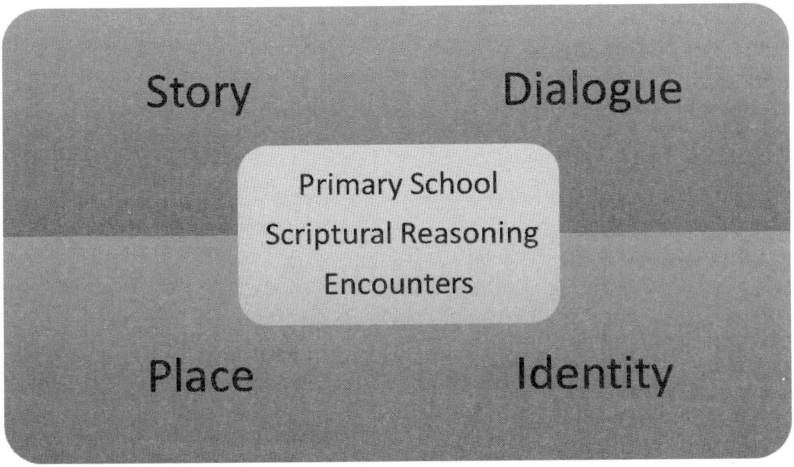

Developing a Framework Within Your Own Context

As I end, I would like to encourage you to take a moment to reflect on what you have read and how these principles might be applied within your own school context. I have tried to set out some of the thinking behind this approach in a way that allows you to translate these principles for your pupils and wider school community. This concluding section aims to raise some ideas that will get you thinking.

Bringing Communities Together to Share Stories

You will probably already be using stories from different religious traditions and worldviews within the RE curriculum. A good starting point would be to carry out an audit and see in which contexts these are already familiar. It may be that you have contacts within the school or wider local community who are practising members of a faith community. They might be willing to come into school, read these stories and engage in a scriptural reasoning encounter with pupils.

Teaching Key Attitudes for Dialogue

Consider including some of the ROC attitudes in your classroom practices. The more children are encouraged to consider other perspectives with respect, openness and curiosity, the more confident they will become. I have also talked about the significance of talking in threes and how the dynamics of a conversation with a third voice allows more nuanced interpretations. Consider building in more opportunities for working in triplets.

Creating Safe Spaces for Scriptural Reasoning Encounters

I have talked about the significance of creating a space for dialogue that signals a different type of encounter. Consider whether there are already any spaces in your school that could be set aside for this kind of encounter. It might involve having a gazebo that you can put up when you want to develop a story-sharing event, or perhaps there is space in the library or an outside area. Consider how you could indicate that this space is different.

Scriptural Reasoning and Identity

Finally, you may want to consider running a scriptural reasoning event in your school.

- Who are the community contacts in your area who might be willing to act as faith guides?
- What theme might fit well with the rest of your curriculum?
- Which stories might be appropriate for the age of pupils taking part?
- How will you encourage pupils to feel confident to share their experiences, in a way that feels safe and inclusive?
- How can you build an environment that celebrates diversity as creative spaces of learning?

Notes

1 See Christian Muslim Forum website: https://www.christianmuslimforum.org/people (accessed 19 July 2022).

2 Cambridge Inter-Faith Programme, 'Scriptural Reasoning', (2016): https://www.interfaith.cam.ac.uk/sr (accessed 8 April 2022).

3 B Koshul and S Kepnes, *Scripture, Reason, and the Contemporary Islam-West Encounter: Studying the 'Other,' Understanding the 'Self'* (New York: Palgrave Macmillan, 2007).

4 Department for Children, Schools and Families, 'Guidance on the duty to promote community cohesion', (2007): https://dera.ioe.ac.uk/8108/ (accessed 19 July 2022).

5 Ssee School Linking Programme website: https://thelinkingnetwork.org.uk/ (accessed 19 July 2022).

6 A Moseley, 'Link Schools Projects—do they build up positive relationships amongst children across different faiths and cultures?' (2011): www.concordant.online (accessed 19 July 2022).

7 A Moseley, 'An inquiry into the development of intercultural learning in primary schools using applied Scriptural Reasoning principles'—Executive summary (2019): www.concordant.online (accessed 19 July 2022).

8 Council of Europe, *White Paper on Intercultural Dialogue: 'Living Together as Equals in Dignity'* (Strasbourg: Council of Europe, 2008).

9 R Kearney, *On Paul Ricoeur: The Owl of Minerva* (Aldershot: Ashgate, 2004) p 5.

10 F C Bartlett, *Remembering: A Study in Experimental and Social Psychology* (Cambridge University Press, 1932).

11 H G Gadamer, *Truth and Method* (New York: Seabury Press, 1975).

12 Commission on Religious Education, 'Final Report—Religion and Worldviews: The Way Forward. A National Plan for RE' (9 September 2018): https://www.commissiononre.org.uk/final-report-religion-and-worldviews-the-way-forward-a-national-plan-for-re/ (accessed 19 July 2022).

13 D Ford, 'An Interfaith Wisdom: Scriptural Reasoning between Jews, Christians and Muslims,' in D Ford and C C Pecknold (eds), *The Promise of Scriptural Reasoning* (Oxford: Blackwell, 2006) p 19.

14 R Jackson, '*Signposts': Policy and Practice for Teaching about Religions and Non-Religious World Views in Intercultural Education* (Strasbourg: Council of Europe, 2014) p 96.

15 D Ford, *op cit*, p 12.

16 G W Allport, *The Nature of Prejudice* (Cambridge, MA: Addison-Wesley, 1954).

17 National Association of Teachers of Religious Education, 'The Shared Space Project' (2017): https://www.natre.org.uk/about-natre/projects/the-shared-space-project/ (accessed 19 July 2022).

18 Theos, *Nobody Stands Nowhere* (animation, 2021): https://www.theosthinktank.co.uk/comment/2021/05/12/worldviews-film (accessed 20 July 2022).

19 Council of Europe, 'Autobiography of Intercultural Encounters', (2011) p 24: https://www.coe.int/en/web/autobiography-intercultural-encounters/autobiography-of-intercultural-encounters (accessed 20 July 2022).

20 J Ipgrave, 'From storybooks to bullet points: books and the Bible in primary and secondary religious education,' *British Journal of Religious Education* (35 (3), 2012) pp 264–281, p 266.